Gidja the Moon

Introduction

Gidja the Moon is *the Aboriginal story that explains the mythological origin of the moon and the role this celestial body plays in the world. Gidja, the Aboriginal moon deity, brought death to the world. This onerous role is shared by the moon deity in many cultures around the world. To the Aboriginal people, Gidja's regular waning and disappearance symbolized death. But Gidja, who apparently dies and indeed disappears, always returns, reborn, to grow once again full, bright, robust. Gidja's predictable cycle of death and rebirth not only marked time, but signified to the Aboriginal's imagination the changing seasons. So Gidja, who is reborn month after month, also represented Nature's annual rebirth after its season of dormancy and rest. It is not surprising that the Aboriginal also saw Gidja as the symbol of the afterlife. They believed that Gidja attends the good gate at the portal of the new horizon, the Aboriginal concept of life after death. No one passes through the good gate without Gidja's approval.*

Gidja lived on Earth during the Dreamtime. The myths of the Aboriginal people spring from this time long ago when human beings were the only living creatures on Earth. The first human beings, who came from the stars, possessed supernatural powers. These ancestral beings brought the world into existence, creating the land and the sea. They brought knowledge, morality, and law. Life on Earth was good in that ancient time until cataclysmic changes rocked the land. Disaster came to Earth in the form of floods, volcanoes, droughts, and earthquakes. Fear moved many of the first ancestors to seek refuge in a most remarkable way. They transformed themselves into animals, birds, plants, insects — and even rocks — as they attempted to hide and protect themselves. It was during this tumultuous time of transition that Dreamtime commenced and the Earth came to be populated with the multitude of life forms we know today.

Dick Roughsey, co-author and illustrator, was an Aboriginal man born on the island of Langu-narnji in the Gulf of Carpentaria. His Aboriginal name was Goobalathaldin. For 25 years, until his death, he and his collaborator, Percy Trezise, worked to preserve the lore of these Stone Age people of Australia. Trezise was privileged to be admitted to the inner, secret and sacred circle of Aboriginal life in 1974. This has special significance, for the Aboriginals guard their lore and will share its complexity only with the initiated. Trezise continues to document the tales he learned through his friendship with Roughsey, both in paintings and through the written word.

Library of Congress Cataloging-in-Publication Data

Trezise, Percy and Roughsey, Dick.
  Gidja the moon.

  (Stories of the dreamtime — tales of the Aboriginal people)
  Summary: After suffering from misfortune and being mistreated by the people
of their tribe, Gidja and his wife and daughter become the moon, the Morning Star,
and the Evening Star.
  [1. Australian aborigines—Legends. 2. Moon—Folklore. 3. Stars—Folklore]
I. Trezise, Percy, ill. II. Roughsey, Dick, ill. III. Title. IV. Series: Stories of the
dreamtime.
PZ8.1.T72Gi   1988   298.2'6'0694   [E]   88-20120
ISBN 1-55532-948-9 (lib. bdg.)

North American edition first published in 1988 by

Gareth Stevens, Inc.
7317 West Green Tree Road
Milwaukee, WI 53223 USA

First published in Australia by William Collins Pty. Ltd.

Editor: Kathy Keller
Introduction: Kathy Keller
Map: Mario Macari
Design: Kate Kriege

1 2 3 4 5 6 7 8 9 92 91 90 89 88

Gidja the Moon

story and art by

PERCY TREZISE & DICK ROUGHSEY

Gareth Stevens Publishing
Milwaukee

Far off in Dreamtime, Gidja the Moon lived by the Yangool River with his people, the Bullanji. Gidja was unhappy. People made fun of him because he had a round, fat face, a fat body, and long, thin legs and arms.

4

Gidja loved Yalma, the Evening Star girl, and wanted to marry her, but she only laughed at him. Gidja decided to sing magic songs to Yalma while she slept, hoping she would dream of him and come to like him.

5

Alone in the bush he made a magic circle of white stones and painted feather poles. At twilight he began to sing:

"Gura Binba Binba, Guraday Lardima Goora Binba, Binba."
"Dream of me and think sweetly of me in your dreaming."

He sang many songs. Soon Yalma could not stop looking at Gidja or thinking about him. The willy wagtail birds, who were always gossiping, saw Gidja and told Yalma that he was singing magic to her.

Every night Gidja sat in the magic circle singing his love songs.
As time passed, Yalma stopped laughing at Gidja and one day
made him very happy by agreeing to become his wife.

They built their bark shelter on the edge of the village. All the Bullanji people held a big corroboree dance to celebrate Gidja and Yalma's marriage.

When Yalma had a baby daughter they named her Lilga, the Morning Star. Gidja loved little Lilga, and as she grew bigger, he always took her with him when he went hunting.

One sad day, when all the lovely wattles and wild flowers were in bloom, Gidja climbed a tree to cut honey from a beehive. Poor Lilga, on the ground underneath Gidja's tree, was accidentally killed when a big tree limb fell down on her.

It was the first time that any of these first people on Earth had died. All the people had thought they were immortal, that they would live forever.

Poor Gidja cried over his dead daughter. But the people were frightened and angry. They blamed Gidja for bringing death to them and began to threaten him with their spears.

Gidja made a bark coffin and decided to bury Morning Star by the beautiful rain forest on the far side of the river. Across the river stretched a vine bridge which kept the people safe from crocodiles when they crossed.

14

While Gidja was crossing the bridge, some men ran to the vine bridge and cut it with stone axes. Gidja, with the bark coffin on his shoulder, fell into the fast-flowing river.

The swift river carried Gidja and the bark coffin away. He cried,
"Help me, I can't swim!" But his people would not help him.
"Serves you right for letting Morning Star die," they shouted.

The river swept Gidja towards the sea. He puffed up his fat body
so he would float. This astonished the pelicans, who watched
Gidja sweep by.

Gidja reached toward the clumps of grass which leaned over the river like helping hands. He caught hold of them and pulled himself out just before he was eaten by a big crocodile.

18

The coffin of Lilga, the Morning Star, drifted out to sea and sank, where it is still seen today at low tide, near the place we call Cape Tribulation.

Because the moon had not yet been created, Gidja knew the world became dark when the sun left the sky. So at nightfall Gidja built a fire for light with the firesticks he had made.

Kookaburras sat in the trees and laughed at Gidja. The willy
wagtails gossiped about him, but the butcher birds sang sweet songs
for little Morning Star.

Gidja carried a burning piece of wood from the fire to light his way through the dark forest. The people saw the light winking among the trees and wondered who was coming.

When they saw it was Gidja, the people were angry again. They thought they had gotten rid of him when they cut the vine bridge at the river.

All the men ran for their spears, and hurled them at Gidja. But the spears just bounced off him as though he was made of stone.

Gidja laughed and said, "You people cannot kill me. I am going to live forever." His big round body shook with laughter at the people who were trying to kill him.

When the people saw they could not kill Gidja, they became even angrier. They caught hold of him and hurled him straight up into the night sky.

As he rose upward into the sky, Gidja angrily shouted down to the people, "From now on, all people will be mortal and no longer live forever. I too will die, but not forever. You will see me come back to life again."

From that night on, Gidja the Moon grows fat and round before fading away again when he looks like a frail, stooped old man just above the dawn horizon.

Not far away is his bright little daughter, Lilga, the Morning Star.
Kookaburras laugh, and dingoes howl when they see the last of
poor old Gidja. And the butcher birds still sing sweet songs to
Lilga.

Gidja is not dead long. On the evening of the third day after he disappears from the sky, Gidja can be seen at sunset, floating there like a baby's cradle, beginning a new cycle of life. Nearby is his wife Yalma, the Evening Star.

As the seasons turn, the grass withers and dies but always springs
back green and alive when the rains come again. Likewise, Gidja
the Moon dies, but always returns to light the night sky for the
whole world.

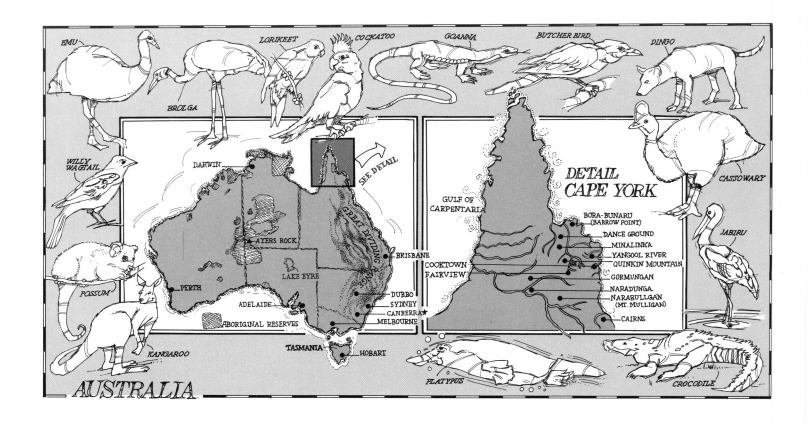

Glossary

Bullanji (bool LAHN gee): an Aboriginal people

butcher bird: an Australian songbird that jabs its food on a thorn or sharp stick to tear it into small pieces

corroboree (ko ROBB bo ree): a gathering of Aboriginal people for sacred, festive, or warlike purposes

Dreamtime: the time long ago in Aboriginal mythology when supernatural ancestors created the world

Gidja (GEEJ ah): the moon, and the father of Lilga

kookaburra: an Australian kingfisher bird known for its harsh call which sounds like human laughter

Lilga (LEEL gah): the morning star, and the daughter of Gidja

wattles: Australian shrubs or trees with spikes or round clumps of yellow flowers

willy wagtail: a small Australian bird whose song sounds like "sweet-pretty-little-creature"

Yalma (YAHL mah): the evening star, and the wife of Gidja

Yangool (yan GOOL): a river in northeastern Australia